"SIMPLY SUPER AWESOME JOKE BOOK

VOLUME I

Jokes, riddles, one-liners and Knock-knock jokes for the whole family!

JOKES!
1

Super High Five Books
All rights reserved

No duplication or copying of anything in this publication
witrhout prior express permission of the author.
©2023

Thank you for choosing this 1st Edition!

Of all the thousands of books on Amazon, you chose this one- and it is truly appreciated!

Although you were likely just looking for a fun, little read, you are also supporting an independent Publisher and his first-ever book.

Thank you so, so much for choosing this book!

Big Joe Kerr

PS. Ratings are the 'lifeblood' of the independent Publisher. A book lives or dies by its ratings. Although you are just starting this book right now, please consider giving it a rating.

Thank you so much!

AND NOW FOR THE TOUGH QUESTIONS...

Step 1: Circle the month (and title) you were born

Jan = The exalted	**Feb** = Captain	**Mar** = Emperor	**Apr** = Bigtime
May = Wild	**Jun** = Big Bad	**Jul** = Ravishing	**Aug** = Hollywood
Sept = DownTown	**Oct** = The Ol'	**Nov** = Lil'	**Dec** = King/Queen

Step 2:
Circle the letter your first name starts with:

A	Ace
B	Buttercup
C	Cheeks
D	Doink
E	Engelbert
F	Fuzzy
G	Goober
H	Grasshopper
I	Booger
J	Jellyfish
K	Porky
L	Loverboy
M	Muffin
N	Noodles
O	Meatball
P	Pumpkin
Q	Q-Tip
R	Rambo
S	Sweetie
T	Tiger
U	Stinky
V	Turtle
W	Whiskers
X	BooBoo
Y	Tank
Z	Nugget

Step 3:
Circle the letter your last name starts with:

A	Fartlek
B	Bonkers
C	ChickenFingers
D	Diapers
E	Extra-Cheez
F	Fartzalot
G	Grizzlefart
H	Hiccups
I	Igloo
J	Dumpybottom
K	Kabobs
L	Cheeseballs
M	McBoingBoing
N	Niblets
O	Onions
P	Phartz
Q	Butts
R	Rumps
S	Smellerton
T	ThunderPants
U	Uranus
V	Von Poopz
W	Weiner
X	Pickles
Y	Bubbles
Z	Zamboni

Step 4: What are the results of the three categories?

1. 2. 3.

So why did we ask you to do that?
Because that is your NEW NAME!!!

Wait...what!?!

We wanted you have to a fun new name...
at least for the duration of this book.
This book is designed to be fun so we
wanted you to have a fun new name to match!

THIS BOOK BELONGS TO
(YOUR FUNNY NEW NAME)

1.

2.

3.

(FORMERLY KNOWN AS)
(THE NAME YOU WERE BORN WITH)

Congratulations on such a beautiful new name. It really suits you.

Would you mind leaving a review on Amazon?

SCAN HERE

Takes you to Amazon

Reviews help indie authors earn an income on Amazon.

TABLE OF CONTENTS

Jokes   8

Knock-Knock Jokes   70

(not so) Deep Thoughts   82

Bathroom Humour   86

Other Stuff   100

Chapter 1
Jokes

Do you know what the drummer named his twin daughters?

Anna 1, Anna 2...

What is the difference between a Hippo and a Zippo?

One is super heavy and the other is a little lighter

What do you call a boomerang that never comes back?

A stick

PRO TIP: Try telling these jokes on elevators they work on so many levels!

Skeletons are actually very fearful
They don't any guts!

What was the Judge yelling when the rowdy skunks caused chaos in the courtroom?

"Odor in the court! Odor in the court!!"

What is red and very bad for your teeth?

A brick

Calm Down!

The insecure, cross-eyed teacher simply couldn't control her pupils

What did the lawyer wear on his first day of work?

His lawsuit

Marvin ordered both a chicken and an egg online.

He just wanted to see which came first

Why don't cows shop online?

They prefer cattle-logs

What do you call a giant
pile of cats?

A meow-ntain

What did the cat on the bottom say?

Get MEOW-OUT!

(Thats what you call a
cat-astrophe!)

What did the cat at
the top of the mountain say?

Nothing- he wasn't much of a talker

The World Tongue Twisting Champ
just went to jail for a loooong time.

He was unfairly sentenced

Do you know why hummingbirds hum?

Because they never
remember the lyrics

What is purple but
smells like yellow paint?

Purple paint.

Do you know what happens when frogs park illegally

They get toad.

How do you get squirrels to like you?

Just act like a nut.

Clerk: "Hey Duck! How are you going to pay for that lipstick?"

Duck: "Just put it on my bill."

Do you know where the Penguin got a mortgage?

At the snowbank

That tiny pony is coughing all the time.

It's because he is a little horse.

What kind of running shoes do Pandas wear?

None- they usually go bear foot.

Rest in Peace
boiling water

You will be mist.

What is worse than finding
a worm in your meal?

Finding only half
a worm in your meal.

Do you know where walls meet?

In the corner…always in the corner.

I made a wooden car
It had wooden wheels
It had a wooden motor
It was perfect except for one thing…

It wooden run.

Reverend Salad always starts church the exact same way:

"Lettuce Pray."

Why does Marvin keep his piggy bank in the freezer

He prefers cold, hard cash.

What do cows stare at
in the night?

The mooooon.

Where do cows
go on dates?

The mooooooovies

What kind of cars do cows drive?

None, silly- cows can't drive!

What animal did the Farmer put in charge of locking the barns?

Tur-keys

Why do birds fly south for the winter?

Because walking would take too long

A napping bull can also be called a bulldozer.

What professionals are actually encouraged to drive away it's customers?

Cabbies and Bus Drivers

Don't ask Military Barbers for directions if possible

They only offer shortcuts

I hate the jokes the Roofers tell

They're all over my head

That poor, dumb bank robber was caught having a bath in the middle of a robbery. He thought that was what a clean getaway was.

My belt is now in jail

Two years for holding up pants

Mona Lisa was sent to prison unfairly

I'm sure she was framed

Hey Marvin, you feeling OK?
You look FLUSH!

JOKES!
23

How did the calf give directions
to his friend to get to his house?

"Its just 'pasture' house and
turn left."

———————

Cows can be really hard to be around

They're often very moooooody

———————

How do you keep a
bull from charging?

Hide their iPhone

———————

JokES!

Why do cows wear bells?

Because their horns don't work

Cows have two horns and provide milk. What has one horn and also provides milk?

A Milk Truck

How do you prevent cows from tipping?

Put them in the stable

Advice for Farmers:

Don't pamper your cows or you get spoiled milk

SPRINTERS NEVER EAT BEFORE THEIR RACES

THEY FAST

If an Alligator becomes a Detective

He's called an Investi-gator.

They mixed a rabbit
and a shellfish.

They named it the Oyster Bunny

If your Big Toe is 12" long,
do you call it a foot?

JOKES!

Farmer: My chickens love Classical music.
All they ever ask for is
"Bach! Bach! Baaaachh!"

I have watch dogs for those chickens
I named them Rolex and Casio G-Shock.

Which type of birds
are heavy breathers?

Puffins!

If seagulls fly over the sea

Are the birds that fly over
the Bay called 'Bagels'?

Which dinosaur has

the best vocabulary?

The Thesaurus!

Giants are very difficult

to understand because

they only use 'big' words.

Earth spinning really makes my day.

The kid across the street made a Pitbull from snow. It had major frostbite.

My sister says she wants to Save the Oceans. But she isn't even willing to help with dishes.

Dad: "Son, what do you want to be when you grow up?"

Son: "A Garbage Man."

Dad: "Why a Garbage Man?"

Son: "Because they just work on Tuesday mornings."

Boy: "Grandpa, why do you have so many books?"

Grandpa: "That's a really, really long story, Grandson."

The Policewoman's three year old toddler didn't want to nap. She could have charged him with resisting a rest.

I really look up to my big Sister.

She is 6'2"!

"MOTIVATION"

Every morning, I see joggers running outside my window.

This motivates me to get up and go close the window.

Balloons have really
gone up in price these days

Its because of inflation

Who can jump higher
than a house?
A Kangaroo or a Tree Frog?

Both! Houses cannot jump.

Mr and Mrs. Burger
just had a baby girl!

They named her Patty.

GERTRUDE WAS FIRED FROM HER JOB AS A CASHIER.

YOGA

SHE KEPT TELLING CUSTOMERS THAT "CHANGE COMES FROM WITHIN"

Horse with wings

A boy showed his Dad a picture he drew of a horse with wings.

His Dad said "You drew it wrong,

Horses don't have wings."

Boy: "Why can't a horse have wings?"

Dad: "Well, if it has wings- then it is not a horse."

Boy: "Well, why did you call it a horse then?"

World's Best Portrait Artist (almost)

Art Critic: I just saw the most amazing portrait artist I ever laid eyes on.

He was actually a Vampire. His portraits were perfect in almost every way- but with one notable exception...

He really sucked at necks.

If a person only draws pictures of trucks, would you call them a

Pick Up Artist?

The Kindergarten Teacher was looking at all her students drawing.

Teacher: "Sally, what are you drawing?"

Sally: "I am drawing a picture of God."

Teacher: "But Sally, no one knows what God looks like."

Sally: "Well, you will see in about 5 minutes..."

Are Sketchers a shoe brand that was meant to be for Artists??

CINDERELLA WAS A TERRIBLE SOCCER (FOOTBALL) PLAYER

SHE WAS CONSTANTLY RUNNING AWAY FROM THE BALL.

What was other reason why
Cinderella was so bad?

She had a pumpkin for a Coach.

Chickens never finish
the games they start.

Too many fowls.

Why do soccer Refs always look so serious even though their job requires them to whistle while they work?

I try to never hang around
with Math textbooks.

They're just full of problems.

I heard Math Nerds want to

get a new cool image.

They now want to be called 'AlgeBros'.

What is the only tool the
Math Nerds, sorry- Algebros- have
in their toolbox?

Multipliers

If a fellow had seven apples in one hand and nine in the other, what would he have?

Huge hands!!

What was the first question that 0 asked 8?

Why do you wear your belt so tight??

If a Hen was good at Math, would you call her a

"Mathamachicken"?

Why aren't there any baseball teams that use a bat for their Team Mascot?

Has everyone overlooked the most obvious choice for a team mascot ever??

"Why do we sing 'Take Me Out to the Ballgame' when we're already there?"

"Why is it called the World Series if only North American teams can play?"

The struggling cake shop and our baseball team has the same problems.

Both need a better batter.

Why was the terrible baseball team hot all summer?

They didn't have any fans.

That new player from Cuba has never scored a run.

I think he is 'homesick".

Frogs would make ideal outfielders.

They are natural at catching flies.

I bought a book on
Cat Obedience Training

I now know why it was in the Fairy Tale section

I didn't know Himalayan cats were so lazy.

But him-a-layin' in the sun all day long!

I was laid off from my job at the cat rescue.
They decided to cut meowers

Could you call an 8-legged cat an Octo-Puss?

Why can I buy cat food that is flavored chicken, fish, liver, duck, beef and even lamb but not mouse??

Call the purr-amedics,
my cat isn't feline well.

My cat likes soda but his
favorites are Meown-tain Dew
and Dr. Pep-purrrr

Cats are so smart.
They only shed
on the fur-niture.

Math Teacher asks Marvin a question

Teacher: If I give you two cats today and one more cat tomorrow, how many cats will you have?

Marvin: Five.

Teacher: No Marvin, listen carefully. If I give you two cats today and one more cat tomorrow, how many cats will you have?

Marvin: Five!

Teacher: OK, lets try this- if I give you two apples and one more apple, how many apples will you have?

Marvin: Three.

Teacher: Good! So if I give you two cats and one more cat, how many cats will you have?

Marvin: Five!

Teacher: How the heck are you getting five!?!

Marvin: Because I already have two cats!!

I have cat-like reflexes
When I see a cat, I instantly like it

The Pirate Cats took over
the ship. It was a Mew-tiny.

People don't know this but
Sir Edmund Hillary used to take
his cat on all his climbs.
'Mittens' was a little
Meow-ntain climber too

I was sleepwalking and
I am sure I ate cat food.

Just don't ask meow

Safari Guide:
    "Did you spot that Leopard?"
Tourist:
    "Don't they come like that?"

Safaris are loaded with con artists
Lion and cheetahs are all over the place!

"I own a cat."

Correction:

You KNOW a cat.

Why do cats only

use laptops?

They prefer trackpads- not a fan of mice.

"My cats' favorite color is puurrple

I am her favorite puurrson

She thinks I am puurrfect

She loves my puuurrfume

She even helped me choose my puuurse.

And she thinks I have the best puuursonality.

She thinks I am both a puuuurky yet puuurplexing puuuurson."

Friend: "I bet your cat even loves your new puuuurrrm hairdo."

"Puuuuurhaps...but I don't think she mentioned that...?"

I can guarantee that my
wife will love Alphabet soup.

But I won't put words in her mouth.

My Mom accidentally added
laxatives to her Alphabet Soup

My Dad now calls it 'Letter Rip".

The Hospital updated
their Donor list.

You could say it's been 'orgnan-ized'.

I went to a new Record Store
for 'Hard-To-Find" albums

Turns out it just wasn't alphabetized and the records were thrown all over the place.

My Mom called my Dad "Cheap".

He got mad, threw his paper plate
on the floor.

Marvin took that job
at the bakery

He simply kneaded the dough.

JOKES!

What do a tiny beaches, very friendly tiny-handed people and kitchens all have in common?

Micro-waves

What can travel the entire globe yet never leave the corner it started in?

A stamp.

That baby monkey is so much like his Dad, he's a chimp off the ol' block.

Traffic lights have no shame- they will change in front of anyone

---

Fun Fact: Teddy bears rarely ever eat dessert.

They're always too stuffed.

History credits a chimp being being the first animal in space.

But didn't a cow jump over the moon long before that?

That fella who uses a clock instead of a belt buckle is a true 'time waister'.

How many loaves of bread can you put into an empty bread bag?

Zero- because if you put any, it is no longer an empty bread bag.

Want to know how to get the stomach to start working?

Just press the belly button.

Why was the skeleton always by himself?

No-body liked him.

What can't Pirates spell?

They tried to learn the alphabet but they keep getting stuck at C.

I trust my blanket more than my bank. My blankey always has me covered.

What part of the face is the only part to go to school?

Pupils obviously

I tried to write with a broken pencil but it was totally pointless

---

Which insect was the first to use the internet?

Spiders- they loved web surfing

Crayons are always jealous of pencils for always being sharper than them.

Two muffins were in the oven
and the first one said
"Whoa- its getting hot in here…"
Muffin #2 said "What the heck?!?
You can talk too??"

I told my Mom that she was

pencilling her eyebrows way too high,

Boy she looked surprised!

I accidentally sold a bunch
of sandpaper to the local
pet store.

All the Google reviews just say "RUFF!"

You don't require a parachute
to skydive.
However, I'd recommend one if
you want to skydive a second time.

Parallel lines have so much in common.
It is such a shame that they will
never meet.

My crazy Uncle has the heart of a lion.
That's why he has a lifetime
ban from the Zoo.

Hill-arious

Definition: Goofy looking mountains

Someone stole my mood ring.
I just don't know how
to feel about that.

I broke a finger last week.
But on the other hand,
I am totally fine.

I can totally see myself
working at a mirror factory.

I took the shell off of
my racing snail.

But all it did was
make him more sluggish.

You can never lose a homing Pigeon.

If you did, then it was
just a regular Pigeon.

Chicken coops only have 2 doors
If it had 4, it'd be a Chicken Sedan.

There was a Prisoner who stuttered and he was an amazing escape artist.

He never finished his sentences.

I asked the Tattoo artist for a sleeve of flames on both arms.

She responded : "First you'll have to get a firearms permit?"

The Art Contest was so close that it had to end in a 'draw'.

An Artist, an Engineer, and a Scientist entered the Doctor's office and sat in a single chair.

The secratary says: "You're early for your appointment Mr. DaVinci."

JOKES!

How many kids with poor attention spans does it take to change a light bulb?

Who wants ice cream??

How many Science Teachers does it take to change a light bulb?

Just one. They are known to be efficient but not known for a good sense of humor.

How many Country music singers does it take to change a light bulb?

Two. One to change it, the other to write about how much they miss the old one.

How many spoiled kids does it does it take to change a light bulb?

None- their Moms do it for them.

How many Influencers does it does it take to change a light bulb?

A team of five. One to change it, one to do her hair, one to do her make-up, one to find a great location to do it and one to take the photos.

How many Wizards does it does it take to change a light bulb?

Just one- and they can change it into anything you want.

We had a bug problem in
my house last summer.

So we formed a SWAT team.

On second thought...

The Teacher asked Marvin where he wanted to live when he grew up.

Marvin: "Massachusetts."

Teacher: "Can you spell that?"

Marvin: "Umm, I think I want to live in Ohio instead."

Sharks are not very helpful

It was a sunny day at the beach and all of a sudden, there were screams:

"HELP! SHARK! HELP!! SHAAARRK!!"

Dumb kid on the beach:
"Why d'ya think he's asking a shark for help??"

How do I fix this?

The Teacher wrote on the whiteboard:
"I ain't had fun this summer."

The Teacher asked the class:
"How should I fix this?"

Marvin puts up his hand and yells:
"Maybe quit being so grumpy all the time!!"

Humpty Dumpty had an awful springtime,

He then had an even worse summer...

I'm curious how autumn went for him...?

The M & M's company fired me.

I lost my Quality Assurance job because I was throwing out all the W's.

Do you know what a Librarian's favorite thing to BBQ is?

Shhhhhhh-kebobs

Bicycles cannot stand up without some help.

It's because they're two tired.

There are two men on bikes.

One is poorly dressed on a tricycle.

The other is a sharp dresser on a bicycle.

Do you know the biggest difference is?

Attire.

How much does Santa pay for parking?

Nothing! It is always on the house!

Do you know how Elves write letters to one another??

They use the elf-abet.

The Head Elf could only Remember 25 letters of the elf-abet though.

He never could figure out 'Y'.

Knock Knock

FUN FACT:

The first person to ever tell a knock-knock joke received the "No Bell" prize.

Knock knock:
   Who's there?
Annie.
   Annie who?
Annie Body home?

Knock knock:
   Who's there?
Isabel.
   Isabel who?
   Isabel not working?

   Knock knock:
     Who's there?
  Figs.
    Figs who?
   Figs the dang doorbell- it is not working.

Knock knock.
- Who's there?

Icy.
- Icy who?

- Icy you in there- now come and figs the dang doorbell!
_____

Knock knock.
- Who's there?

Ice cream.
- Ice cream who?

- ICE CREAM AT YOU TIL YOU OPEN UP THIS DOOR!!!

_____

Knock knock.
- Who's there?

Scold.
- Scold who?

- Scold out here! Please let me in!!

Knock knock.
> - Who's there?

Lettuce.
> - Lettuce who?

- Lettuce in, we said its freezing out here!

Knock knock.
> - Who's there?

Ferda.
> - Ferda who?

- Ferda last time, just let me in!!

Knock knock.
> - Who's there?

Water.
> - Water who?

- Water you waiting for? Open this dang door!!

Knock knock.
> - Who's there?

Tank.
> - Tank who?

- Tank you for finally letting me in.

Knock knock.
> - Who's there?

Ida.
> - Ida who?

- Ida know why you took so long opening this door.

Knock knock.
> - Who's there?

Nana.
> - Nana who?

- Nana yo business why I took so long!

Knock knock.
    - Who's there?
Canoe.
    -Canoe who?

- Canoe please just answer the door next time?

Knock knock.
    - Who's there?
Hatch.
    - Hatch who?

- Gesundheit! (or 'Bless you")

Knock knock.
    - Who's there?
An interrupting frog.
    - An interrupt---

    - RIBBIT!!

Knock knock.
- Who's there?

Needle.
- Needle who?

- Needle little help getting this door open.

Knock knock.
- Who's there?

Spell.
- Spell who?

- Sure! W-H-O! Easy!!!

Knock knock.
- Who's there?

A little old lady.
- A little old lady who?

- I didn't know you could yodel!

Knock knock.
> - Who's there?

Owls go.
> - Owls go who?

> - Yes, thats correct.

Knock knock.
> - Who's there?

Iran.
> - Iran who?

> - Iran here as fast as I could. I gotta sit down now though, I am tired!

Knock knock.
> - Who's there?

Iraq.
> - Iraq who?

> - Iraq'd my brain why I just didn't get a ride, I wouldn't have been so tired now.

Knock knock.
> - Who's there?

Dozen.
> - Dozen who?

- Dozen anyone think my new haircut is nice?

Knock knock.
> - Who's there?

Thermos.
> - Thermos who?

- Thermos be a better way outta here.

Knock knock.
> - Who's there?

Razor.
> - Razor who?

- Razor hands in the air like you just don't care.

Knock knock.
- Who's there?

Olive.
- Olive who?

- Olive with my parents and my cat.

Knock knock.
- Who's there?

Candice.
- Candice who?

- Candice be the last knock, knock joke?

Knock knock.
- Who's there?

Shore.
- Shore who?

- Shore would be nice to have a few more knock, knock jokes. Lets do a few more...

Knock knock.
    - Who's there?
Stopwatch.
    - Stopwatch who?

- Stopwatch your doing and come outside to play!

Knock knock.
    - Who's there?
Robin.
    - Robin who?

- Robin you, sucker! Give me your wallet!

Knock knock.
    - Who's there?
Alex.
    - Alex who?

- Alex-plain why I turned bad later! Now give me that wallet!!!

Knock knock.
- Who's there?

Amish.
- Amish who?

- You're a shoe? I never would have guessed that!

Knock knock.
- Who's there?

Avenue.
- Avenue who?

- Avenue ever been asked for a hug before?

Knock knock.
- Who's there?

Armageddon.
- Armageddon who?

- Armageddon sick of these knock-knock jokes. Lets move on to something else.

(NOT SO) DEEP THOUGHTS

(NOT SO) DEEP THOUGHTS
82

Deep thoughts:

Don't you think all cemeteries should be on dead end streets?

Deep thoughts:

Don't you think people with one arms should get a discount at Second Hand Shops?

Deep thoughts:

Do you think Noah used flood lights on his Ark?

Deep thoughts:

Do you think a soldiers least favorite month is March?

Deep thoughts:

Do you think one a beaver is done his work, he exclaims "Dam!"?

Deep thoughts:

A wise man once told me "He who goes to bed with itchy bum wakes up with stinky fingers".

Deep thoughts:
What if skunk farts didn't smell bad?

Deep thoughts:

Do triangles think circles are pointless?

Deep thoughts:

Do you think if a fly didn't have wings, they'd be called 'walks'?

Deep thoughts:

Do you think if two plates go out for supper together, they'd always say 'dinner's on me?"

Deep thoughts:
Do donuts have sweet dreams?

Deep thoughts:

Getting hit in the face with a soft drink still really hurts.

BATHROOM JOKES

WARNING: PROCEED WITH CAUTION
Only the immature should proceed.

PROCEED AT YOUR OWN RISK

This last chapter is guaranteed to be totally immature and borderline inappropriate.

But it will be funny! So if you are fine with that, keep on reading :)

Dedications:

This chapter is dedicated to 'Pee'.

You'll always be my #1

This chapter has lots of poop and pee jokes.

No jokes about constipation though.

We just couldn't get those out.

BATHROOM JOKES

What is the difference between a Pub and an elephant fart?

One is a Bar Room
and the other is a
BaaaaROOOoooommm!

"Hey Buttcheeks- you look tired."
"Oh boy- I am so wiped out!!"

Did you know Ghosts will never unplug a toilet?

No- they try to scare the crap out of it instead.

How was that?
Still feeling OK?

That is about as rowdy
as things are going to get

If you can handle those jokes,

you'll be fine with the rest.

Carry on...

Who wins every race between:
Turds vs Farts?

Always Farts!

They've been blowing away
competition for years!

Do you think after Woody
farts, he says

"Darn tootin'!"

I am so loyal
to my toilet

We've been through so

much crap together.

The Perfect Crime:

Someone stole the toilets from the Police station but got away with it

The Officers had nothing to go on.

Patient: "Doctor, I don't understand what a bladder infection is?"

Doctor: "Oh oh, urine trouble!"

There is a new plumber at the Space Station

His name is

Flush Gordon

BATHROOM JOKES

Knock Knock

Whose there?

Anita

Anita who?

Anita poo!
Where's your bathroom??

Knock Knock

Whose there?

Police.

Police who?

Police flush after you're done pooping.

These jokes stink!

BATHROOM JOKES

"Christopher Robin! Why do you stare into the toilet?"

"Oh, I am just looking for Pooh."

The guy was so embarrassed that he fell off the toilet. You could tell because his his cheeks were red.

What is invisible but smells like Carrots?

Bunny farts

BATHROOM JOKES

I have a book I keep in my bathroom
where I write all my most personal thoughts.

I call it my 'diaryhea'.

Why are people in the Army so good
about flushing after pooping?

They were told it is their duty/doodie.

My top two reasons to not
drink from the toilet

#1   and   #2

I keep walking in on the Pterodactyl in the bathroom.

Why?

Couldn't hear her in there.
The P is silent.

———————

It doesn't matter where you were born, whenever you are in the bathroom,

European

for those few minutes

———————

I dropped my watch in the toilet while taking a poop.

Talk about a crappy time.

———————

Drunk guy:

> "I have to poop. Be right back."

Minutes later...

"ARRRRGGGGHHHHHHHH!!"

Friend: rushes to find his friend
> "What is happening?"

Drunk guy:

> "Something keeps squeezing my butt when I try to flush."

Friend:

> "That's a mop bucket, you fool! You're in the Janitor's closet."

Ode to Toilet Paper

Its never truly appreciated until its gone.

What breed was that little brown dog in the bathroom?

It was a Poo-dle

Do you know why they don't use toilet paper to construct elevators?

Because they'd only go to the bottom.

Where do sheep pee?

In Baaaaaaa-throoms

Do you think Superman calls his toilet the "SuperBowl"?

Why is there cake, presents and balloons in the bathroom?

There was a birthday potty

BATHROOM JOKES

How much do farts weigh?

Nothing.

If they weight anything, they are no longer considered a fart.

My fiancee requested that I wouldn't fart in front of her at least until after we were married.

It made for some wild wedding vows!

King Tut and his son had identical smelling farts.

You could say they had a 'Toot-in-common'.

Pro Tip: Next time you fart- yell 'Turbo Boost' and walk faster.

You're done :)

_____

Did you have fun reading this book?
If you had fun, please review it.

Why?

Because it truly helps an Indie Author get noticed on Amazon (and continue making books)..

Takes you to Amazon

SCAN HERE

THANK YOU!

THANK YOU

One last thing….

Do you like
FREE STUFF?

Please go to our website and sign up for our FREE road trip games & weekly jokes. We'll also update you on our next joke book whixh we are already working on.

Or just go to:
SuperHighFive.com

_____

Please stay in touch!

THANK YOU

Made in the USA
Monee, IL
01 March 2023